FOREPLAY & FELLATIO:
200 TIPS TO MAKE YOUR **LOVER MELT**

THIS IS A CARLTON BOOK

Text and design copyright © Carlton Books Limited 2007

This edition published in 2008 by
Carlton Books Limited
20 Mortimer Street
London W1T 3JW

Material in this book has previously appeared under the titles *How to Give
a Mind-blowing BJ* (Carlton, 2007) and *The 100 Best Foreplay Tips Ever!*
(Carlton, 2007).

ISBN 978 1 84732 214 2

Printed and bound in China

Senior Executive Editor: Lisa Dyer
Senior Art Editor: Gülen Shevki-Taylor
Design: Anna Knight & Tim Pattinson
Production: Kate Pimm

FOREPLAY & FELLATIO:
200 TIPS TO MAKE YOUR LOVER MELT

LISA SUSSMAN

CARLTON
BOOKS

contents

THE **100** BEST
FOREPLAY
TIPS
EVER!

Section One

Warm-up Moves

Foreplay isn't just a little pre-entertainment before the main event. It's what puts the "oh, ohh, ohhh"! in your big O's. You get more blood flowing from the extremities of the body toward the parts that need them and a heightened sensitivity all over. Get enough of the stuff and even a light caress on your wrist can make you throb.

One problem: Because your average guy is basically good to go from the moment he wakes up in the morning, it's thought that foreplay is a special little something he does for you. Not so. A recent study proves that guys ache for a little pre-sex action. However, because his body has a different setup (notice the penis?), many women really don't know the little touches that get his pulse pounding. Read on for how you can both get the bedroom build-up you crave.

Must-do Smooches

Nine dishy, gotta-have-it-now lip locks to lay on each other right now. Pucker up!

Alternate between deep teeth-gnashing, lip-bruising French kisses (for him) and light, feathery kisses (for her).

Don't just go mouth-to-mouth. Throw your whole body into it. Cradle his face with one hand and grab his bottom with the other while grinding your breasts and pelvis against him.

3 Master this tongue teaser: While making out, wrap your lips around his tongue and suck, starting slow and soft and gradually building up to fast and stiff. It'll feel like you're making love to his mouth.

4 Kiss each other some sweet place you never have before.

5 Pack a more powerful erotic punch by not-quite kissing him. Hover above him, gliding your lips over his, but pulling back the second he tries to connect. Repeat a few times before going in for a deep smooch.

Time yourselves. Kissing for at least 20 seconds twice a day (the average relationship lip-greets only ten seconds a day max) will keep your passion motors in overdrive all day.

7

According to Tantric text, a woman's upper lip has an energy channel that connects with her clitoris. When kissed just right, it can start a sexual bonfire that burns through both your bodies. To spark things, he should kiss your upper lip while you kiss his lower lip (FYI, reversing this arrangement has a cold-water effect).

Men like their foreplay hard and heavy. So make him drool with these five lip-licking smack downs.

- Tug his bottom lip with your teeth

- Lightly suck his tongue when it's in your mouth

- Nibble at his neck

- Tickle the roof of his mouth with your tongue

- Cup his head and pull him toward you to deepen the kiss.

9

Your lip action tips off your lover how you'll be in the sack. So avoid the following kiss-offs.

- **Tonsil Snorkelling:** A little tongue action is good, but not so much that you feel like you're choking. Stay to the front of the mouth.

- **Sucking Face:** It's called snogging, not noshing. Swallow to keep your saliva at a juicy but manageable level.

- **Being Steadfast:** Good for commitment, but not such a hot kissing trait. Keep moving using different motions and amounts of pressure – slide your lips over each other's faces, use your tongue to dart and swirl, and keep your hands moving.

- **Peckers:** Unless it's a quickie, plan on more than just 30 seconds of continuous bussing to really heat things up.

Five Instant Turn-ons

Tips that will get you both in the mood to – ahem – get in the mood. Surprise – you'll be fully clothed!

10

Talk the talk. Memorize the following phrases and use at your own carnal risk.

- Caress your lover's cheek, lock eyes and utter three simple words: **"I want you"**.

- Any email longer than **"CU Later"** will keep you on each other's brains all day and make it easier to slip into some one-on-one action when you are F2F.

- Scream, **"Boo"**. Scaring each other stimulates the neurotransmitter dopamine in the brain, which can trigger your sex drive.

- **Give a compliment.** It will make your lover feel noticed, special and appreciated, and closer to you… all of which add up to him feeling more inclined to make you feel good in bed.

- Saying **"I don't need to answer that"** if your mobile or pager goes off while you're together guarantees an orgasm later.

Caress the tresses. Each hair follicle has its own sensitive nerve. Sink your fingers in, lightly pull the shafts up and away from the scalp and they'll feel it right down to their curling toes.

Pick up a pair of furry handcuffs (available from sex shops like **www.annsummers.com, www.libida.com and www.sh-womenstore.com)** and pass them to him under the table at a restaurant, saying "Here's a little something for later." He'll be asking for the bill before you finish your sentence.

12

Work from the bottom. Take turns **massaging** the length of each other's legs, from the **upper thighs** down to the **ankles**. Then focus on the **feet**, kneading the **heels** and all other points beneath. Last of all, zero in on the **toes**, stretching and sucking them individually.

13

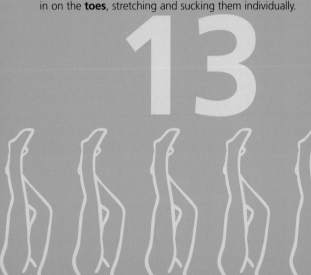

14

Cooking together heats up more than the kitchen. Whip up an easy sophisticated cheesy snack (sauté asparagus stalks in olive oil for three minutes, sprinkle with Parmesan, salt and pepper) that's packed with zinc, a key mineral needed for getting and **staying lusty**. Add a clove of crushed garlic if you want to boost blood flow to special places. Follow with a wicked chocolate dessert and you'll load up on phenylethylamine, a neurotransmitter that activates the brain's pleasure centre, and caffeine, which can jolt your **sex drive**. Start feasting.

Never underestimate
the heating power of
a great big bear hug.

16

Put on lipstick in front of him. He'll start fantasizing about your lips and what he wants them to do. Better yet, let him put it on your lips for you.

Fair Play

His 'n' her get-busy-in-a-jiffy basics that'll deliver mind-blowing results.

17

Yes, you could just speed ahead to grabbing his penis and pulling to turn him on. But it's so much more fun for him (and you) to dawdle and diddle in the slow lane. Here are five slow-mo moves that might get him arrested for sexually loitering.

- Get him to take a deep breath. Whatever activity he's attempting (World Championship Ironman or your own personal iron man), deep, regulated breathing will help him stay in control without losing his will. When he feels like he's burning out, he should stay very still, relax his genital muscles, and take a long breath in through his nose for a count of five seconds and hold it for two before slowly exhaling through his mouth for six seconds. He'll be able to stay in peak condition for as long as you want to play.

- Go ahead and bring him to the brink. Then ignore him. It's a guaranteed way to send him into a frenzy... and swell his orgasm later.

- Trick him. Get this close to his naughty bits with your mouth and then pass right on by. To really make him twist and burn, blast some hot air into the area.

- Indulge your inner dominatrix. Position his body how you want it or, if he makes a move to head down below, pull him back up if you're not ready. Being the object of your sexual attention will bring his entire body to a fever pitch. He doesn't have to ask for what he wants or worry about how he's doing performance-wise. And playing Mistress means you get the kind of stimulation you need, when and where you want it.

- Don't forget: You have a whole body there – not just 6 in (15.2 cm). Spend at least an hour tracing the outlines of his frame with your fingertips without saying a word.

18

You can only speed things up so much. Study after study shows that women need at least 15 minutes of foreplay before they're good and ready to move on both mentally and physically (in addition to having do-me-now urges, she needs to start lubricating and her vaginal canal must expand to handle his – er – abundance). These five moves will rev your engine. Don't be shy – most men are willing and eager to do whatever it takes to please their bedfellow.

- Pick up some female-friendly porn like the *Black Lace* or *X Libris* series to read together. Besides getting you hot under the collar, the torrid prose will give him lots of sizzling ideas for bawdy things he can try with you.

- He can send you into a tailspin simply by spiralling his fingertips along your forearms, neck, the palms of your hands and any other sensitive body spot. The circular motion is much more intense than the usual up-and-down straight line rub.

- Don't beat around the bush about requesting oral. It's the shortest, fastest route to paradise for most women (a fluent cunnilinguist can bring a woman to orgasm in minutes).

- When in doubt, kiss. Women get immense erotic pleasure from frequent, lusty, passionate make-out sessions. Just remember that this does not always mean frantically wrestling tongues. Try to mix up your lip play with the occasional oh-so-seductive butterfly peck on the nose, eyes, forehead and other body parts.

- For a heart-racing sensation, have him almost-caress you by holding his fingertips just above your skin and running his hands over your naked arms, breasts, belly and thighs so they just brush those fine body hairs. Mmmm.

Section Two

Lose Your Senses

Too often, touch is the only sense that takes centre stage when you're doing the passion rumba. But bringing all of your senses into the experience will transform your foreplay from nice-but-basic to a full mind-body, haul-out-the-fireworks fantasia.

Every type of sensory stimulation, from the sight of your lover's naked body to the sound of their voice whispering in your ear to the potent smell and taste of their skin turns on parts of the brain responsible for getting your buzz on. Read on for the tantalizing secrets that'll make you feel like the ultimate sensual seductress. You can use these tips to focus on one sense at a time or create a combo platter that treats several senses at once. Don't expect to be of sound mind once you're finished.

Surround yourself with these sexy sounds...

- Say something. Anything. Even if it's "Uhhhh". If you're not up to expressing your own pleasure, a bare-bones string of four-word phrases whispered in the heat of the moment can work wonders. Try, "Do you like that?" or "Does that feel good?"

- So you want a little foul-mouthed foreplay? Good. But it's only sexy talk if you're speaking the same language. Sit opposite each other, point to your bits and decide together what you're going to call them. Clothing optional.

- You don't have to have a dirty dialogue to make things hot. Just breathing each other's names every once in a while between the "Yeahs" and "Ooh, babys" here or there is proof that you're what's making your lover feel so good (and that you remember who you're in bed with).

- When it comes to making sheet music together, some tunes rap out a sexier beat than others. Any number that has you toe-tapping faster than the human heartbeat (about 72 RPMs) will arouse your doin'-it desires while slow-beat scores like those found in reggae, Latin or Barry White songs will send good vibrations throbbing through your lower body.

- Talk in public. Plant yourself in a crowded place (on a blanket in a park, at a club or party, in a busy restaurant) and whisper your fantasies to one another, sparing no racy detail. You can do something about it later, when you get home.

- Let the foreplay begin on your drive home. Call your lover and say you've been thinking all day about having a passionate, steamy encounter with them. Or tell them you'll meet them at a specific time in the bedroom with no clothes on.

20

Savour these tasty treats…

• Before tongue diving between their legs, swish with a minty mouthwash for 30 seconds. It will make your tongue feel tingly good on their nether regions and make them taste fresh as a stick of gum.

• Order the tasting menu. There are so many yummy flavours of lubricant and edible body products (see tips 12 and 68 for resources) now available, why settle for just one? Dab different flavours of lubricant strategically over your different erogenous zones and have your sweetie nibble your skin to discover them one by one. They'll soon be searching your body for more!

• What you eat can make a big difference to your pre-blow-out action. Here, a hungry girl's guide to working some food into your foreplay.

Drizzle each other with champagne and lick it off as it fizzes on your skin.

A sprinkle of cinnamon down there will wake him up like morning coffee.

On a hot night, lick the salt off each other's sweaty bodies.

Hunt the sweet spot. Dab a little honey or chocolate syrup on your body and then challenge your lover to find it using only their tongue.

Get juicy by rubbing a sticky fruit like papaya or mango all over each others' bodies and then licking each other clean.

Take a can of whipped cream to bed with you. Enjoy.

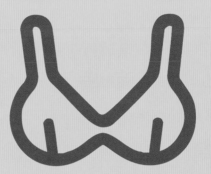

Use the following to put on your own
private peep show.

- You don't even need to touch him. Just seeing you do
  some sexy thing injects an instant shot of testosterone
  into his bloodstream. Put him on guard by locking
  eyes with him. Then reach under your shirt, arch and
  unclasp your bra. Wriggle it free and toss it toward
  him. He'll be all over you.

• Men like to see naked women. But if you don't feel comfortable putting on a strip show, have him undress you, slowly, and caressing and kissing each part of your body as it comes into view.

• Stay in the spotlight. Leave the lights on, light a few candles or get busy in the daylight hours.

• As you play, pull back your hair so he can see what's going on.

• Set the action in front of a mirror so you can both watch.

• Watch a skin flick with the sound off (it's actually much hotter when you lose the stilted horny workman-smutty housewife dialogue).

22

The nose is connected to the limbic system of the brain, which controls libido. Seduce it with these intoxicating scents.

- Certain floral aromas can trigger sexual arousal. Put a couple of drops of rose, jasmine and ylang-ylang oil on the light bulb in your bedside lamp, switch it on and get turned on.

- Spray a touch of his cologne on the sheets. One study found that women who fantasized while smelling a popular men's cologne were more aroused than when smelling women's cologne or a neutral odour. If he doesn't have a signature scent, shop for one with him. That's foreplay, too.

- Raid the pantry. Research shows that guys turn into lust-crazed beasts (or similar) at the smell of cinnamon buns, lavender, vanilla, doughnuts and pumpkin pie (interestingly, french fries and beer didn't make the list). Women also get off from sniffing lavender and pumpkin pie, as well as liquorice and cucumber.

- Perfuming your lower stomach is a much more effective aphrodisiac than spraying your wrists. As you become aroused, blood flows to the pelvis, generating heat and releasing the fragrance. Try something with spicy tones, which has been shown in studies to have a boosting effect on his penis.

- Skip the perfume altogether. One study found that men who sniffed vaginal secretions are more likely to find a woman attractive than men who took a whiff of water.

Thrill each other with these tantalizing touches.

• Take a steamy shower together... with the lights out.

• For extra shower power, make it a threesome: Pour a couple of drops of shower gel into a spray bottle and mix it with water. Spray each other, then rub. You'll feel three different types of stimulation – the steady pelting of the shower, the soft spray of the soapy gel and the firm caresses of your lover's mitts.

• There are parts of your body that are so seldom touched that they are, by default, especially sensitive. Discover yours by touching each other using any part of your body – your hair, your feet, your lips – except your hands.

23

- When it comes to foreplay, men and women crave distinctly different finger moves. Women get turned on by softer, gentler caresses while men typically want things hard and harder. Take turns giving each other a sensuous gender-customized stroking. He can use a feather to lightly trace tingly touches over your skin while you can limber up your hands with oil to give him a deep penetrating rubdown all over his body.

- Avoid these touchy-feely moves:

    Scratching anywhere near his boys with inch-long talons

    Rubbing him down with patchouli, rose, jasmine or any other girlie-scented oil

    Pinching, punching or anything that will leave bruises

    Jamming his boner so hard it cracks

    Tickling him until he pees in his pants.

Section Three

Feeling Feverish

Your skin is jam-packed with 45 miles (72 km)
of sensitive nerves that are often ignored as you
head toward your more guaranteed pleasure
launch locations. But caressed the right way
these oh-yeah zones will deliver a mega jolt
to your sex play. (Yes, that goes for men, too.
The male body is so much more than his little
bobble-headed mate.)

Check out the tips in this section to find out how to travel beyond the usual hot spots to explore some erotic locations on your body that you probably won't find in your average sexual tour guide. Pack some massage oil and let the voyage of carnal discovery begin.

Your Pleasure Map

Don't leave home base until you read this.

24 When using your hands, keep them both in constant motion to maintain the experience at high-pitch.

25 Instead of working your way through your bodies following your usual head-to-toe map, go off-road and jump from spot to spot, moving your fingers, lips, tongue and stick shift in erratic patterns instead of a straight line. Never knowing where you're going to touch next keeps every nerve he has constantly on the edge.

26 Warning – some of these body parts don't often see the light of day so make sure they all pass the sniff test (places to wield a washcloth and soap: behind the ears, between the breasts, the belly button, underarms, the top crease of the bottom and the toes). According to one study, good grooming counts even higher than penis or breast size with some lovers!

Everyone has their own specific sequence of caresses that turns them from docile playmate to a sex maniac. Here's a no-hassle way to access each other's code: Lie together naked (sounds like fun already, doesn't it?) and take turns trying different touches on your bodies. Give each fondle a number between one and ten, depending on how good it feels. When you get really good at this, you can say, "Give me a number ten and make it snappy!"

Play in the zone. Getting as close to tried-and-trues without actually touching them will make you wiggle and wriggle for more. By the time you actually cross over their erogenous borders, the sensation will be that much more earth-shaking.

Head Rush

Here are five heady touches to the noggin.

29

Firmly roll the edge of the ear between your forefinger, middle finger and thumb, going back and forth from lobe to top.

30

Find the pulse point (around 1¼ in / 3.5 cm under the earlobes and just under the jawbone) and, using three of your fingers, rub tiny circles with very light strokes. If you're doing it right, you should feel their pulse start moving faster than a train).

31 To release endorphins and get your lover in the mood, use your tongue or finger to lightly probe the ultra-sensitive skin behind the ear.

32 Stimulate the auriculogenital reflex (ear-stimulation response) by heavy breathing into the ear. Some people find it so exciting they actually climax from it.

33 Give him an eye-opener by lavishing his lids with dry, light kisses. Finish by gently breathing hot air over his lashes.

Go Neck-in-Neck

Try these five steamy ways to neck-it.

34

Give goosebumps by kissing the back of the neck very softly.

35

Devour, suck and nibble at the soft skin where the neck meets the jawline.

36

Men's neck skin tends to be thicker than yours, so use your whole mouth to suck on his skin. Or alternate sucking with gently biting a path up and down his neck.

If you want to leave your mark, suck in one spot hard. Ambidextrous vampires can use their tongues to caress and soothe the bruised skin at the same time.

37

Brush your lips between their throat and chin where the skin is thinner so the nerves and blood vessels are closer to the surface.

38

Second-hand Information

Arm yourself with these seven handy wanton touches.

The skin on the inside of the elbows is chock-full of close-to-the-surface nerves. To make their body tingle, run your forefinger from the palm to the crease of the arm and linger there for a bit.

40

There are 40,000 nerve endings in each of the palms just waiting to be tickled, teased and tantalized. With your fingernails, lightly scratch small, gradually widening circles into the open palm until you're tracing the outer edges of his palm.

41

Run the pads of your fingertips up and down their outstretched fingers.

42

Flick your tongue quickly in and out of the centre of the palm.

43 Give your lover shivers by licking their wrist and then blowing softly to create a cooling sensation – special receptors there are tuned to detect differences in temperature.

44 Slowly, lightly stroking their hand from the palm up toward the fingertips will kick the area's touch receptors in gear and awaken other parts of their body.

45 Gently suck on and lick their armpit.

Middle Ground

Two luscious tactics for the treasure chest.

46

Anyone can maul breasts like a porn star, but it's the superstar lover who knows to trail a wet line between your breasts.

47

Meet chest to chest and press.

Belly Love

Press the button with these two racy moves.

The area between the belly button and pubic bone is packed with pleasure points. To arouse them all, massage, lick or nibble the soft skin from the navel down to where the pubic hair begins.

48

Belly orgasm. Take turns sitting erect on the edge of a chair with the other person standing behind. The one standing places their hands in a triangle on the sitter's abdomen, pointing downward, and rubs. The person on the receiving end will soon feel a sexy buzz building up.

49

Side-by-Side

No one is going to give you a red card for performing these two off-side penalties.

50

The skin from underneath the armpits to just above the hips is one long orgasmic runway. Take off using long, slow, continuous strokes with the palms of your open hands, circling at the hips and coming back up to where you started. If you're causing more giggles than sighs, then you're working too shallow and too quickly.

51

Gently tongue and nibble along the melt-down inner crease where the elbow meets the upper arm.

Back-up

Get their back up with these three dishy strokes.

52 Gently rubbing the base of the spine will send shivers up their back and way down below.

53 The small dent just above the crease of the bottom (aka "the sacrum") is absolutely packed with sensitive nerve endings. Use your fingers to rub its surface and around its edges. The harder the better, so don't be afraid to put your whole body into it.

54 As you get lower down the back, the nerves become more sensitive. Work the whole area by gently kneading the muscles between the shoulder blades and spine, and then immediately following up with light fingertip strokes.

Leg-it

Master these three heavenly steps.

55

Because of its out-of-the way location, the back of the leg from the knee down to the ankle rarely gets touched. But the skin here is so thin that all it takes is a little continuous stroking to make your lover weak at the knees. Use the backs of your fingers and fingernails like a feather duster, delicately brushing the area with light up-and-down strokes. Avoid a tickling sensation by following up with a firmer touch to stimulate the pressure-sensitive nerve endings, called the Pacini's corpuscles. Alternate hands to keep the motion constant.

The inner thighs are ultra-quivering to touch. They're also the home of the lymphatic system, which releases chemicals that cleanse the body of toxins. Which is why kneading a handful of the soft flesh in this area can create a pleasant buzzy state.

57

Using both hands, start at the hips and caress the flesh working your way toward the inner thighs. Now trace the same line with your mouth. Repeat this alternating sexy build-up until he can't take it any more (you'll know because he'll push your head toward a more central between-the-legs region).

Toe the Line

Here are two caresses that'll get your feet wet.

Lather your hands with some massage oil and, applying pressure with your thumb, trace a line from the top of the big toe down into the valley between it and the second toe. Continue up the second toe and so on, repeating the movement all the way down to the little toe.

59

Give his tootsies a soaking by gently sucking the toes, from the big one down to the little one. Finish with a tongue swirl over the hyper-responsive in-step.

Section Four

Spicy Hot, Hot, Hot

You've tried different positions, various locations, and new hotspots in your bedroom play. Now it's time to turn up the heat and try a walk on the wild side. Here, for your pleasure, is a selection of just-this-side-of-kinky ways (no dog collars or whips included) to take your foreplay to the edge. Thrown into your repertoire, these moves will add spice, boost your connection and deliver some down-and-dirty instant gratification.

One note before you strip down: Never introduce something out-of-the-ordinary without a little build-up first. Make it sexy by waiting until you're both naked and heated (i.e., when your partner is more likely to let you have your wicked way) and whisper, "Wanna try something different?" Even if they don't go for what you have in mind, you'll find out what their definition of "kinky" is. Now use that knowledge for good… and go blow your mind.

Hair Today, Gone Tomorrow

Experiment with better grooming.

While there are salons that will make you smooth as Sinatra, you can shave the hair off yourself. Think buzz cut, not bald. Remove it all and you'll soon find out why you have pubic hair: It prevents skin burns. Concentrate on the sides and the areas down below.

There are five basic options for taking it off. You'll need a mirror or a partner with a steady hand for all of them.

- **Shaving:** Condition your hair first (it makes removal easier) and use a sharp razor, scissors or an electric shaver to shape your hairline into whatever pattern you like.

- **Depilatories:** Spread the cream on thick, wait five to ten minutes and rinse. Watch out for clogged drains.

- **Waxing:** Put waxed strips where you want to take it off and – youch – strip! A good pick if you're considering a little S&M experimentation with your partner (you being the "M").

- **Brazilian Bikini:** A more intense version of waxing that also removes hair from the inner thighs, buttocks and sometimes the entire pubic region. Double youch!

- **Electrical or Laser Treatments:** You need a pro for this one as your hair will be removed permanently with special equipment. Not for those who change their mind easily!

Instead of a complete shave with a razor (which can leave an itch), trim each other using electric clippers. **Bonus:** The extra buzz can trigger an orgasm.

62

If he isn't sure about giving his forest a prune, tell him that the shorter the pubic hair, the bigger his organ looks.

63

Watch and Learn

Whether it's viewing some raunchy porn action or watching your lover getting off, a little knowledge is a wonderful thing.

Don't act like you caught him cheating if you discover him in a self-embrace. You want a lover who's comfortable working his own pleasure. Here's why...

64

- According to studies, people who masturbate are more likely to get off when with someone else. So their self-fulfilment will make you seem like a better lover.

- Your lover is also more likely to be in the mood in two shakes. That's because all the action boosts hormone levels, especially testosterone and oestrogen, which primes a woman by producing wetness.

- If your partner knows how to work their own buttons, they can train you more easily (and teach you some cramp-relieving shortcuts).

Take one step beyond and let your lover watch as you get acquainted with yourself (or tag team each other).

65

Don't just watch: Do! Getting in on their act may make your lover feel more comfy about showing all in front of you. Try giving them your hand and asking them to guide it over their body, however feels good. Or ask to put your hand on top of theirs.

66

67

Make them feel like they're part of a threesome – while they self-service, stroke another bit of their body.

68

Watching porn can also give you some insider info to the opposite sex. But it will not produce the desired results (white-hot blinding lust) if your naughty video of choice features a seriously clueless bimbo, who keeps getting banged by big men out of the blue or lots of naked men and women sitting around talking. Pick a couple of friendly flicks (check out the user-friendly rating system at **www. goodvibrations.com** and **www.evesgarden.com**).

Getting the Vibe

Get ready to swipe the batteries
out of your TV's remote control.

Some vibrators shake, rattle, roll and even lick. But if
you're shopping for the dream his-'n'-her machine,
opt for something that fits in the palm of your hand,
such as a finger vibrator, mini bullet or pocket rocket.
It'll produce the same power vibes as a mega version
without freaking out either of you over its size (see
tips 12 and 68 for resources).

70

Give him something to buzz about. Strap him into a vibrating cock ring (tips 12 and 68 tell you where to buy) and hold on tight for his orgasmic blast-off. If you really want to send him into the stratosphere, position the vibrator lower down behind his ball bearings.

71

Work the sides. The pulsing sensation from a vibrator can be too intense for direct contact on sensitive bits. Start at your outermost extremities, pushing down hard. Moving in tiny circles, work your way in, gradually letting up on the pressure so that by the time you reach the bull's eye, the vibrator is barely touching the skin.

Don't get lazy: It's not just that little guy by himself but the sexy combo of you and your battery-operated mate that sends your partner into seventh (or even eighth) heaven. Here are four ways to work together to get the best orgasmic results.

- Run the vibrator over your partner's nipples while you lick below.

- Team up down under – alternate using your mouth and your buzzing buddy.

- Make it feel like an orgy by working your other hand into the mix.

- Rub the vibrator along parts of their body that you don't usually think of as sexy and see how fast you revise your opinion.

73

Here are four things that are better than a vibrator.

- **Kissing.** Lips meeting, teeth-knocking, tongue -ashing kisses are the stuff that love is made of (check out tips one to nine for great suck-ups).

- **Using your tongue.** The two great things are that it's soft and wet. Your vibrator is not.

- **Nipple sucking.** Many woman (and men) can get off just from having their chest knobs kissed.

- **A warm body.** Sure, your Mr Buzz may be able to go all night and into next week without stopping, but will he cuddle you after?

Adjust Your Thermostat

Playing with temperatures can make lukewarm lovemaking sizzle.

Adding heat to the right spots has a knock-on effect of literally raising your body's temperature, causing blood flow to increase, which in turn makes your skin more come-hither to touch. End result: You're screaming, "C'mon, baby, light my fire." Be warned – a little heat goes a long way. Here's how to get things smokin'.

- Blow. Warm breath on the skin raises its temperature. Head for less obvious thin-skinned spots like the earlobes, neck and inner thighs.

74

- Work up a slow burn by gently massaging a small blob of heat-activated lube (check out tips 12 and 68 for where to buy) all over his penis. The longer you rub, the warmer it gets.

- Sip some hot water, but don't swallow. Instead, carefully swallow him. The heated liquid will bring him to boiling point.

- Dribble warmed-up (finger-test the temperature first) honey, chocolate or syrup over their body and lick off.

75

Adding a frosty touch to your foreplay can actually make things hotter because it energizes your nerve cells. Here's how to add thrills with chills.

- Ice him. After working his body into a sweat, run an ice cube from his neck all the way down one side of his body, up the inside of his leg (but staying away from his heat stick), down the other side and back up.

- Crank the mercury back up to heatwave numbers by doing the above, but hold the ice cube in your hot little mouth this time.

- Fill a condom with water and freeze. Peel off and instant, presto, you have a dildo lolly to play with.

- Make an ice cream sundae out of their body. Don't forget the cherry on top.

76

Blow hot and cold. Done in succession, these two sensations pack a one-two wallop to your orgasms. The easiest way is to lick a small area and then blow hot air on the wet patch. Even better is to use booze because the alcohol evaporates more quickly than water, so it creates a cooler effect when you blow.

Playing Rough

Think of these moves as tough love. Remember to establish a safe word before you start in case you want to put a stop to things mid-action.

Get hard on him. He's the stronger sex, so he can take it. Pinch his nipples (an often-overlooked nerve centre), scratch your nails down his back, massage his chest, knead his bottom, squeeze his boy parts. He'll get off on your girl-gone-wild manhandling.

78

A little love tap on the bottom can add some power to your foreplay. Remember that his bottom is not your boss's face, so use a light touch. First, prime the area with some rubbing. When you do finally smack, keep your hand relaxed and slightly cupped so it's more of a caress than a stinging slap. Run your other hand between his legs at the same time and you'll soon see what a naughty boy he can be.

You could invest in locks, Velcro or special ties, but go for a more soft-core approach that doesn't require too much preparation other than clean linen. Take turns wrapping each other in the bed sheet so the arms are pinned but the head, shoulders and lower legs uncovered. Now kiss every inch of exposed skin. The helpless sensation of only being able to receive pleasure can be very addictive.

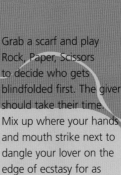

Grab a scarf and play Rock, Paper, Scissors to decide who gets blindfolded first. The giver should take their time. Mix up where your hands and mouth strike next to dangle your lover on the edge of ecstasy for as long as possible.

80

Section Five

Melt-down Moves

To really give your foreplay a blood-pumping jolt (and make the mattress springs squeak), you need to get out of your routine and strut your stuff into titillating new territory.

But that doesn't mean you should ditch what works. After all, those tried-and-true moves are the makings of orgasms. Nor must you risk arrest in a public place (unless you want to).

It does mean injecting a little of the unexpected into the proceedings, however. So if the last venture you made out of your safe zone was longer than a month ago, it's time to read through these melt-down moves and discover your hidden turn-ons.

Mix It Up

Repetition is great for learning the multiplication table, but it doesn't do much for your sex life. According to an Archives of Sexual Behaviour study, just doing one thing differently can tally up your foreplay pleasure. Here are new ways to liven up your standard repertoire.

Learn the formula: If an area gets too much continual stimulation, it gets desensitized. Three minutes is enough to keep things interesting before moving on.

03:00:00

Here are four new techniques that will make him want to give you a round of applause (not to mention return the favour – tell him to study tips 84 to 85).

82

- Vary your type of touching: Switch from circles to side-to-side swipes.

- Polish his knob. Grease your hands with plenty of lube. Palm the head of his penis with one hand, pressing down and moving in tiny circles. Meanwhile, joggle the shaft with your other hand.

- Stop the action in the middle of a handjob and tickle the underside of his penis with your fingers or a feather.

- Lace your fingers together and wrap them around his piston. You can move up and down, twist back and forth or combine the two while squeezing to work him into a tailspin.

83

Three games for playing ball with him.

- Don't just grease up his bat. Squirt some lube between your hands and gently rub it all around his testicles.

- Wrestle his testicles into joyful submission by gently tugging on them.

- Get him to sit up and beg by using your finger to lightly scratch the underside of his balls.

84

Four fresh moves he can try on your clitoris. Be warned:
You may accidentally promise to become his love slave
after he performs these on you.

• Most men do
wrong by the clitoris because they
go for a heads-on rubdown, which can
actually be painful (probably not the sensation
you're hoping for). For more sati-sighing results, have
him gently play with the tip or rub a finger along the sides.

• Your clitoris is a very sensitive soul. Make sure it doesn't get
manhandled by having him switch-hit between rubbing, stroking,
licking and sucking, varying the amount of pressure he applies.

• You need lube, too. Even if you make your own juice, a spritz of
water-based lubricant on your nub will heighten sensation and
cut down on the friction that can rub you the wrong way.

• Getting him to lie perpendicular to your body
means he can stroke or lick you crosswise
rather than the usual
up and down.

Teach him to read your lips with these
three lessons in love.

- Packed with nerve endings, the labia are so
  much more than a pitstop on the way to the
  vagina. Have him hold each one between his
  thumb and forefinger and massage it, working
  his way up and down.

- His finger is not a stand-in for his penis. So once he
  does gain entry, he shouldn't start jamming back and
  forth. Much more sexy is if he crooks his hands so that
  he can slip one finger in and wiggle it ever-so-slightly
  about while using his thumb to wag up and down
  your outer bits (if he's got long digits, he may even
  be able to reach your joy button).

- Get him to gently pull back your labia
  as if he's opening curtains so that your
  entire love region is exposed. He can
  now work his thumb and tongue over
  and under and all about.

Three nifty ways to become bosom buddies
(men have nipples, too).

- Lightly lick the outline of the nips
  in smaller and smaller circles until
  you have just the point in your
  mouth. Swirl with your tongue
  and reverse the sequence.

- Pucker your lips around
  the nipple and suck so
  that your mouth forms a
  seal. Ante up the pressure
  by inhaling and exhaling.

- Remind him that there is so
  much more to your breasts
  than the gumdrops on the
  top. Get him to caress and
  lick the sensitive top, bottom
  and sides of your breasts
  before coming in for a
  nipple landing.

86

Moan Zones

Enter at your own orgasmic risk.

GET INTO HIS ZONE:

87

- Flirt with his fraenulum, the bundle of nerve endings just on the underside of the penis where the foreskin attaches to the head. When you're working his penis with your hand, squeeze a little extra pressure from your fingers directly on this spot with every downward stroke. Have a tissue handy for unexpected explosions.

- Hit his U note. The urethra is the tiny area of tissue above the opening (yes, it's the some spot where his pee comes). Press it lightly and he'll liquify.

- Walk his line. The raphe is the ridge that runs lengthways along the scrotum. Trace your fingers along it to the tip of his penis. Try not to fall off.

PUT HIM ON YOUR TIME ZONE:

- Have him give you the finger. This is the best move for pushing your G-spot (a soft swelling that lives halfway up the front wall of your vagina that will make you scream with joy when pressed). He should slide his thumb up about 2 in (5 cm) and press hard as if he were trying to make a thumbprint on the front of your vaginal wall.

- Say Aaaah! Studies show that merely finger stroking your anterior fornix zone (located on the front wall of the vagina between the G-Spot and the cervix) can juice you up and multiple orgasms.

89

ZONE OUT TOGETHER:

• Patch things up. The perineum (the passion patch of skin between your respective treasure chests and backsides) is made from the same sensitive tissues as your other sex organs. Rubbing a finger right there, light and fast, will make you both squirm.

• Get bummed. That tiny little hole is actually crammed with spine-tingling nerves. You don't have to go in deep; a well-lubed finger pressing around the outer regions is all it takes to cause a melt-down. If you do want to go in further, make sure your fingers and the entire area are clean and well-lubed.

Double Play

Get twice as turned on by divvying up
your moves between two different spots.

You'll make him feel like he's part
of a lusty ménage-à-trois when
you work both of your hands on
different points of his body at the
same time. Keep one hand around
his love stick while using your other
hand to scratch his inner thighs,
balls or to stroke his bottom.

91

Work one hand between the legs while sucking on your lover's finger at the same time, using the same moves with your tongue as your digits are using down below. Your lover won't know if he's coming or going.

Get him to button you up by lightly tapping with his tongue or finger on the top of your clitoris while caressing the top of your bottom where the crease ends.

92

93

You'll go ga-ga when he slides one finger inside of you while gently rolling your love kernel between the thumb and forefinger of his other hand.

94

Give each other some skin. It's the largest sex organ on the body so the more you touch it, the better. While you're squeezing each other's other organs, rub your feet together and up and down each other's legs, push your bellies against each other and wriggle your pelvises. Get in touch wherever and however you can.

Lightly bite your lover's nipples (this goes for him, too) while touching down below. Expect sparks.

95

96

Turn his penis into his eleventh finger. Grasp it at the base and slowly rub it over your clitoris. At the same time, reach behind and work your fingers against the rim of each other's rear entries. Bliss off!

97

Get him to give you a full working over inside, outside and through the back. He begins with a sweet circular stroke to your love bud. Once you're feeling fine, he crooks his forefinger into a "come hither" position and slips it inside of you to tap lightly against the G-Spot. While tapping, he substitutes his tongue for the finger working your genital blossom. This frees up that hand to gently rotate around your back garden. Don't be surprised if you promise a BJ a day for the rest of his life in the heat of passion.

The Big Bang

How to know when they're going to blow…
and what you can do about it.

Two ways to get a cue:

- Moans, gasps and cries of "Oh my God, I think I'm gonna come" are generally good indicators that you've got a good thing going.

- Someone starts issuing "Uh, a little to your left. Ooh, a little to the right. Higher – no, higher" instructions.

Three signs he must ignore:

- Your love buzzer goes into hiding. When she's close to climaxing, the clitoris retracts beneath the hood.

- You're not getting juicy. Lubrication depends on so many things – your hormones, your cycle, your diet. So how much motion lotion you're making is not a good indicator of how ready you are to rumble.

- You become very still. You shouldn't mention this too much because he gets jealous, but women are capable of coming again and again. So when you first freeze, chances are you're riding your first orgasmic wave.

99

Not ready to call an end to your play? Try these six tricks to get him to stay in the game for as long as you want.

- Add a chill – such as an ice cube or wet towel – against the small of his back to distract him long enough to regain control. Cold shower, anyone?

- To keep his tongue from getting tired, he should try sticking it out, closing his mouth around it and moving his lips and nose to work your bits.

- To give him a second wind, lay him down flat. This will stop the blood flow from springing his love gun back into firing stance.

- If he starts dribbling, let him go. He's reached the point of no return and risks straining or even tearing his urethra in his attempts to squeeze back the flow.

- If he's regularly trigger happy, help him put his safety lock on by holding the shaft of his penis in your hand, firmly squeezing for ten seconds and then releasing.

- Slip on a condom. A love glove helps keep him in check. A desensitizing gel may slow things down, but you risk transferring it and numbing your own happy regions.

Ready for the grand finale? Here are seven things you can do right this minute that guarantee orgasm. Hold on to your hat!

100

• Give yourselves a hand. If you need to seal the deal quickly, try mimicking your body's pre-orgasm movements. That means cupping his testicles in your hand and gently pressing up toward his body while you clench and release your PC (pubococcygeus) muscles (the same ones you use to control your pee flow).

• **Teach his fingers to figure skate.** Instead of working your clitoris in an up-and-down motion, have him trace around it as if he were drawing an "8" over and over and – mmm – over. By constantly varying the degrees of pressure between hard and soft, he'll soon put you into a layback spin.

• **Mix it up.** When your orgasms are stuck in a rut, shake things up by moving in slow motion or shifting things up to fifth gear.

• **Push his eject button.** Keeping a steady pressure on his prostate (see tip 87) will launch his load in seconds.

• Hold your breath. When you climax, you experience a toe-curling head rush. Multiply that by 1,000 by holding your breath for five seconds just as you start to gush.

• Get him to keep 'em coming. Take a brief pause for intermission and then resume the action. But because you're bits are ultrasensitive, he should gradually ease off on the pressure after each body rush.

• Have him multiply. This doesn't mean he's going to keep on erupting. Orgasm is the moment when your pelvic muscles pleasurably contract at the peak of a sexual experience and similar in men and women. Ejaculation is a lower–spinal reflex that expels semen from the body. When you sense his fuse is about to blow, use the safety lock techniques in tip 99 to help him regain control. Then rapidly work him up to the brink again. With enough practice, he'll be captain of his penis, able to command it at will to orgasm without losing any of his erection-strengthening love juices.

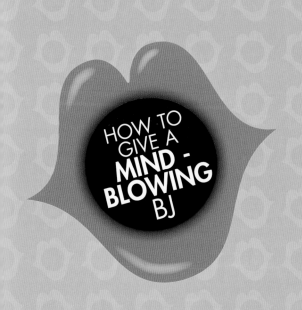

Section One

Oral Studies

It's a no-brainer to say that men are suckers for blowjobs. According to *The Hite Report*, almost all the 7,000+ men polled listed fellatio as their hands-down most beloved sexual past-time. Which is why it's unfortunate many women don't have the first idea how to handle his favourite tool. They grab, fumble and give up. But here's a little secret: The reason he rates blowjobs so highly is because to him your mouth feels like your vagina with a brain. So read on for your below-the-belt guide to giving him some smart lip service.

Have you ever seen a grown man melt?
You will.

Director's Cut

One thing – depending on where his penis hails from, he may still be wearing a turtleneck (America is one of the few countries where the men are circumcised for non-religious reasons). The foreskin (a loose fold of skin that covers the glans or the head of the penis) doesn't always stretch back and allow full access once he's erect, so check out the uncut version of the tip for getting under his hood.

Basic Bobs

Tongue-whipping his penis into a frenzy isn't complicated. Follow these basic seven steps blow-by-blow for mind-searing oral sex he'll love to get and you'll love to give. Remember, practice makes perfect.

1

Lose the fear.
The average
guy's equipment
is a manageable
3½ in (8.6 cm) turned
off and 5½ in (13.7 cm)
turned on.

2

A little enthusiasm goes a looong
way. More than an incredible body
or a great technique, what gets
him going is knowing that you truly
want his penis in your mouth. So
before you even get near his fly, let
him know how thrilled you are to
get on kissing terms with his little
guy and not just doing charity work
("Please, please can I go down on
you?"). Contrary to urban legend,
most men take longer than a boiled
egg to get off. Expect to spend at
least ten minutes down there.

3

Take care removing the merchandise. Most zipper injuries (just reading these words will make many men cringe) occur on the un-zip when less attention is being paid. (Extra goddess points for unzipping him with your mouth.)

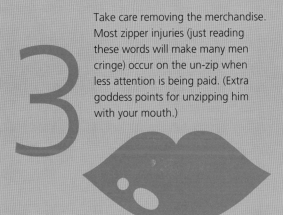

However you arrange yourselves, never force a good penis down once he's up. Putting downward pressure on an erect penis strains the suspensory ligaments, the two long tendons that give him the wherewithal to become stiff in the first place. Stretched too far, they'll lose their spring which will result in an erection that may permanently point down instead of up. The key is to strike a pose that has him moving upward into your mouth. Read on for a slant on the top four pole positions you can take.

4

- **Call Girl:** One of the most popular, he stands up or kneels and you crouch between his legs with your head at the level of his crotch.
  Ups: You get plenty of freedom of movement to show off your stuff.
  Downs: He can control the thrust and depth. Put your hand at base to stay in the driver's seat.

  - **69:** This is a great position where you can both give and receive at the same time by lying down facing each other with your heads at opposite ends (variations on the theme: he's on top and you're on bottom, vice versa or you lie side by side).
    Ups: You get as good as you give.
    Downs: Since you're both caught up in your own blissfest, you never get or give all that much. Much better is to do a 6/9 where you take turns taking care of each other.

- **Lying Down, Part One:** He's flat on his back and you're kneeling over him.
  Ups: You are in total control.
  Downs: None, actually.

- **Lying Down, Part Two:** You're flat on your back and he's ducking and diving over you.
  Ups: He gets plenty of feel-good depth.
  Downs: He gets plenty of feel-good depth. Try lying with your head slightly hanging over the edge of bed. While he essentially stays in control of the thrusting, your throat will now be opened wide enough to be able to take him in without gagging (plus it looks porn-star sexy).

- **Sitting:** He lounges on a chair or sofa with you next to him, bent over his bounty.
  Ups: This is a good position for a relative beginner as the limited range of movement means he can't thrust up into your mouth.
  Downs: You can't take that much in your mouth once you become more adept. Change positions so that you're kneeling between his legs instead of bowing over them.

5

Cover
your teeth
with your lips.
The odd nip here and
there is fine, but he doesn't
want you to treat his delicate tool like
an ear of corn. Along the same lines, don't
play rough (unless he asks for it). Yanking back
the foreskin, sucking too hard, pumping up and
down like you're trying to draw water from
a dry well and snagging any part of it on
jewellery (including mouth studs) are
all no-no's.

Start
slobbering. The
wetter things are down
there, the better. Always have
some water nearby in case you get
cottonmouth (check out tips 33
to 38 for more on keeping
things juicy).

6

7 Squeeze the shaft of his joystick with one hand to keep him steady and slide your (very) wet mouth over it until your lips meet your hand. That's it. Don't suck – or blow, for that matter. What you (and he) want to start with is a slow up-and-down movement that rubs against the sensitive skin of his penis.

Uncut Version: Don't take him out to play just yet. Instead, moisten the area around the foreskin; then gently edge your tongue under the hood and swirl it around before sliding it down. You can then either hold it down at the base of the shaft or pump it up and down the shaft. BTW, his penis is not a microphone. So don't speak into it and ask how you are doing. If he is enjoying himself, his moans will give it away.

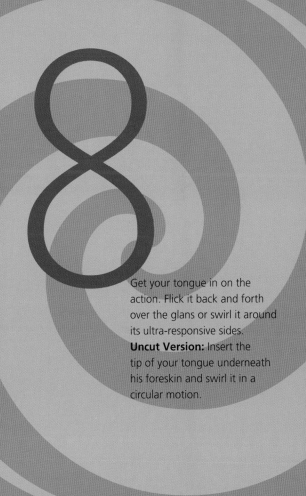

Get your tongue in on the action. Flick it back and forth over the glans or swirl it around its ultra-responsive sides. **Uncut Version:** Insert the tip of your tongue underneath his foreskin and swirl it in a circular motion.

Keep in rhythm.
Start off slowly so
every movement is
exquisite torture;
only pick up the
pace as he gets
ready to explode.

9

Get monotonous.
Though your mouth
may feel as if it's about
to fall off, keep steady
and keep on suckin'.
While lots of variety is
good at the beginning,
don't change your mouth
moves once you get him
to the edge or you may
have to start all over from
scratch (see tips 69 to 71
for more on giving him
a blow-out finish).

10

Cold Start

Don't worry if he's as flabby as an old lady's triceps when you start your play. You'll his penis into a hard body lickety split with these buff moves. One word of caution before you begin: Wait until he's fully ready to play before starting the heavy tackles. If he thrusts his penis before it is fully erect, he risks bending and buckling injuries, which could end up benching him for the season at best and possibly leaving him with a painfully perpetual bend when he gets erect.

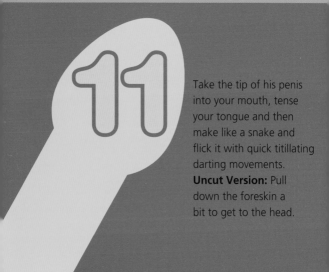

Take the tip of his penis into your mouth, tense your tongue and then make like a snake and flick it with quick titillating darting movements.
Uncut Version: Pull down the foreskin a bit to get to the head.

Warm him up with this simple move. First, gently take him into your mouth to get him wet from head to base and then dry him off by gently blowing your hot breath over the entire area.

12

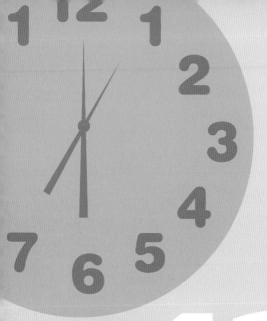

Take your time. A series of pit stops that tickle and tease will have him springing to attention before you even get near his cylinder. Kiss and lick around his inner thighs, his testicles and then slowly up his shaft toward the gland. Once there, tickle the area with your tongue until he's in high gear.

Come Up For Air

Beginners at fellatio tend to hold their breath. But you don't want to pass out before he does. Here's how to breathe without disrupting the action.

14

Whatever his size of tool, you'll be able to take it in your mouth if you exhale before you take the plunge. Here's how it works: When you inhale and then hold your breath, your throat becomes like an inflated balloon, pushing your tongue and the back of your mouth higher. But when you exhale and then hold your breath, the vacuum in your trachea pulls the back of your throat lower, adding up to 2 in (5 cm) to your capacity.

15

Try breathing through
your nose.

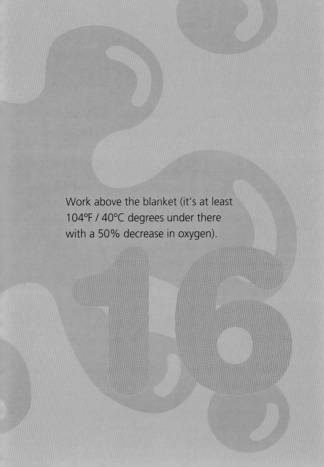

Work above the blanket (it's at least 104°F / 40°C degrees under there with a 50% decrease in oxygen).

Mouth Drills

If you've been doing sit-ups and lunges in order to impress your loverboy, you've been working the wrong muscles. Instead, try some simple stretching exercises to keep your tongue and sucking muscles limber and strong. Repeat each of the following exercises ten times.

- **Go Fish:** Push your lips all the way forward, rolling the insides out and then opening and closing your mouth much like a guppy.

- **Spin the Bottle:** Tie a string around the neck of a half-filled large bottle of water and lift it using just your lips.

- **Air Lip:** With your mouth firmly closed, push the air upward so that your upper lip blows out. Hold for three seconds, then release.

- **Tongue Yoga:** Stretch your tongue out as far as it will go and try to touch first your nose, and then your chin.

- **Lip Wagger:** Circle your tongue around your lips in a clockwise motion and then reverse the motion to counter-clockwise.

- **Buy a Body Double:** Get a double-decker ice-cream cone and slowly lick all around it. Then put the whole mound of ice cream in your mouth. When it starts to drip down the side of the cone, use your tongue to catch the drops.

18

Sexpert-approved tricks to prevent mid-action injury.

- Go "up" on him instead. Kneel on the floor so that his head and shoulders rest on the floor or bed, his back angles toward your stomach and chest and his bottom rests at your neck level. Then wrap your arms right below his hips to support him. You'll seem strong as a weightlifter, but it's gravity that's really doing all the lifting.

- Strategize. The more you prepare the field before you tackle his tackle, the less time you'll need to spend in an oral scrum-down. So go offside and work him up with some clever hand moves (see Section Two: Tickle His Pickle for ideas). When he's about to score, up the action with some easy oral plays. Run your tongue up and down his shaft to lubricate him, use the tip of your tongue to trace a trail around the base of his penis or gently suck on his balls as you move your hand up and down his shaft, kiss your way along his member, flick your tongue against the nerve-packed fraenulum (that little ridge on the underside where the head meets the shaft). At the last moment, take him fully in your mouth.

- If your jaw gets tired mid-action, switch to licking and kissing his penis and/or stimulating it manually.

- Use a chin rest. Put one pillow beneath his hips and another under your chest. His lower back will be more relaxed, and it'll be easier for him to adjust his knees and legs, allowing for more sensation. Prop your chin on your fist, with your pinkie down, and use a finger to put pressure on his perineum (the magic bit of flesh between his balls and bottom). Watch him hit the roof.

Getting Into Shape

Sighs do matter so match your mouth play to his penis shape and size.

Monster Dick: If he's on the large size, don't be heroic and try to choke up all of him at once. You'll just end up spitting him right out again. To stop him from rear-ending your tonsils, have him lie on his back as you crouch over his crotch. That way you can pull back if he pushes in too deep. Best of all, you'll leave your hands free so you can use them on the boys. As he grows to full size, lick the length of his penis, alternating between sweeping up-and-down strokes and circular motions. When you're ready to take more of him into your mouth, try this gag-proof technique: Lick or lube your hands (study tips 34 to 38 for which lubes to use). Then form a tube with one hand and put it against your lips. Wrap your mouth around his shaft and slide your mouth and hand up and down in unison.

Uncut Version: When his appendage is on the XL size, his extra layer of skin may not retract completely. If you want more of him to work with, gently push it toward the base of his shaft.

Short Dick: If he comes in a mini, make the most of what he's got by taking the whole thing into your mouth and sucking hard. The tight fit will make him feel like he's driving a stretch limo.

Uncut Version: Make him feel like the biggest man in the room by holding one hand in an L position firmly at the base of his penis, pulling the skin back from the base (in the direction of his pelvis). Not only does it make him look bigger, but it also heightens sensitivity. You may have to peel back the loose folds of skin to get at his good stuff.

20

Fat Dick: Yes, it's sweet when you can gobble up his entire sausage. But it isn't really necessary to stuff yourself. Since the most sensitive part of his equipment is in the first 1½ in (3.8 cm), you can still give him a tongue lashing by concentrating your energies there. Swirl your tongue around the ridge where the head meets the shaft; then gently suck the tip.

Uncut Version: Beware of bunching. You can flatten any lumpy bits with a light push of your hand.

Section Two

Tickle His Pickle

Employ backup. Don't make the mistake
of thinking oral sex is like soccer in that
the use of hands is not permitted.
If you only use your mouth, you risk dishing out
the world's longest blowjob. Not because your
mouthwork isn't seductive and steamy, but because
most men enjoy (and often need) extra stimulation
to intensify and speed up their joyride to bliss.
Master these multitasking tips and he'll love you
for your carnal coordination.

Get A Grip

Start with the basics – here, six steps to perfecting your handshake.

Which hand do you write with? Then make sure that paw has easy access when you deliver the goods or you may end up with worker's cramp (with no guaranteed compensation).

Lick your hand. Unlike women, men don't have built-in lubricants. If you use your new extra-strong grip on him dry, you'll probably give him carpet burn (tips 33 to 38 will whet your appetite with more ideas on how to juice him up).

To perform a workaday, no-frills handjob (which will still plaster a goofy grin on his face), firmly but gently grasp your hand around the base of the penis and slide it upward until it reaches the head. Then rub your palm over the head in tiny exquisite circles. Slide your hand back down to base camp and, adjusting your hand so your palm is squeezing the opposite side of his pole, repeat the move. Continue, making each upward squeeze last at least ten seconds. After every fifth upward squeeze, throw in a quick, firm, up-and-down pump stroke.

25

When in doubt, press even harder. What would make you writhe in pain will make him writhe with delight because his skin tends to be tougher and thicker than yours. If you're not sure how hard, have him give you a hands-on demo of how he likes to touch himself, and then follow his lead.

26

Once you have the basics down cold, throw these make-his-toes-curl handholds into the mix.

- **The Tickler:** Make his Mr Happy even happier by lightly tracing your fingers over the entire area.
- **The Big Squeeze:** Press your palms flat against the sides of the shaft and press hard while moving your hands up and down.
- **The Corkscrew:** Squeeze the head of his penis and gently wiggle it back and forth while holding the base with your other hand.
- **The Kneader:** Hold his baguette so that your thumbs are touching. Lightly pull in opposite directions and then come back together.
- **The Ring:** Encircle just below the head of his penis with your thumb and forefinger and pump up and down with it.

27

Do any of the above in public and he will worship at your feet.

Flicking Him Off

Easier than patting your head while rubbing your belly, using your hands and mouth on him at the same time will make him feel like he has the starring role in a ménage à trois.

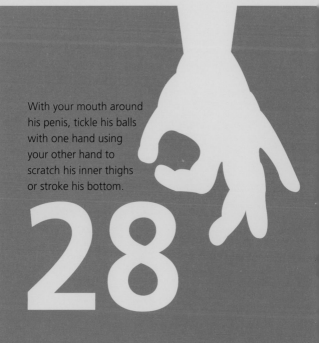

With your mouth around his penis, tickle his balls with one hand using your other hand to scratch his inner thighs or stroke his bottom.

28

Prick his prick. According to acupuncture, there are meridians – interconnected channels of energy – running through the body. To get in touch with his amorous avenue, pop him into your mouth while pressing the base of his big toe with the heel of your hand. Follow-up with a rub along the top of his foot and up the inside of his leg. When you get to his inner thighs, slow down and lighten your pressure to fingertips only while you trace around his testicles and his tummy, ending up on his chest.

29

30

Sometimes a subtle unexpected pressure makes the difference between a fan-sucking-tastic session and a blah one. Here are three jabs he wants you to give him.

- Use your thumbs to press lightly on the sides of his shaft while your tongue does the talking.
- Squish hard against his perineum with your thumb, moving it in tiny circles.
- If you're game and he's down, put your (well-moistened) pointer in his rear (slowly, gently!).

31

Give his hot rod a rub 'n' shine. Tightly grasp his shaft in your hand just below the glans and slightly twist while using the flat of your tongue to swirl just around the rim of the head.

Use one hand to guide his penis into your mouth, and then, looking him in the eye, reach up with both hands to tweak his nipples.

Slippery When Wet

Women have (rather handily) built-in lubrication systems, but men don't. So a little extra lube can go a long way toward juicing up your erotic escapade.

33

Squirt stingily; being too generous removes friction (what his penis thrives on). Squeeze one drop on the palm of your hand and one on the tip of his rod and get steamy.

Uncut Version: You probably won't need much lube since the ultrasensitive skin is covered by the foreskin.

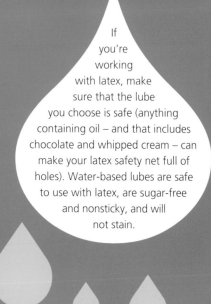

If you're working with latex, make sure that the lube you choose is safe (anything containing oil – and that includes chocolate and whipped cream – can make your latex safety net full of holes). Water-based lubes are safe to use with latex, are sugar-free and nonsticky, and will not stain.

34

35

Merge two favourite hobbies – eating and sex – with yummy-flavoured lubes. There are chocolate creams to satisfy your sweet tooth, champagne and strawberry dick lick drops and fruity oils if you don't like your treats artificially flavoured. Check out the lube selection at sex shops such as www.blowfish.com and www.annsummers.com.

36

Make like a wild scientist and sexperiment. Some lubes list glycerine or cinnamon, peppermint or clove oils in the ingredients. When you smear these on his skin and blow, his hotdog will heat up to boiling point. Others contain benzocaine or other mild anaesthetics that numb the skin and trigger an amazing sensation when they wear off. (Heads up: The deadening action means you may also be sucking on his lollipop for a long, long time.) Check out tip 34 before using.

37

Want to feel like a natural woman? Then drizzle him with Bodywise Liquid Silk or Astroglide, lubes which most closely mimic your own natural body secretions (see tip 35 for information on where to buy).

Accept no substitutions. Do-it-yourself lubes such as deodorant, hair gel, body lotion and petroleum jelly can cause chemical burns on his most sensitive bits. Follow this rule of thumb: If it's safe to eat, it's probably safe to smear on his dick (honey, ice cream, butter, yogurt, syrup and cheese spread are a few buffet examples – but skip anything spicy like salsa or mustard). Check tip 34 for protection issues.

33

Propping Him Up

Send the amorous action to new heights by adding a few toys to your oral play (see tip 35 for shop-til-you-drop sources).

Get a buzz on the next time you dive between his legs.

- Use a finger vibrator on his balls, perineum and rear hole.
- Slide a slimline vibrator behind his balls.
- Rest your chin on top of a wand vibrator.
- Hold a small vibrator against your cheek.

39

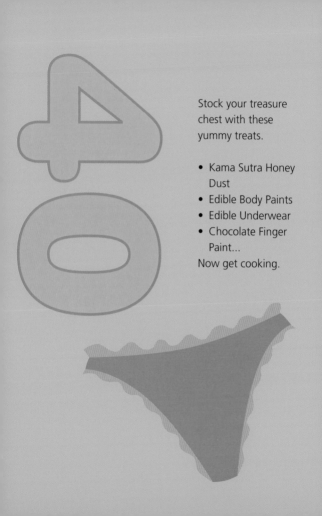

Stock your treasure chest with these yummy treats.

- Kama Sutra Honey Dust
- Edible Body Paints
- Edible Underwear
- Chocolate Finger Paint...

Now get cooking.

41

Want to express your inner erotic artiste? Dip a soft-bristled paintbrush in frosting or chocolate syrup and use his groin as your canvas. Then devour your masterpiece.

Wrap a silk scarf or a strand of love beads around your hand and slide it up and down the shaft and head of his penis.

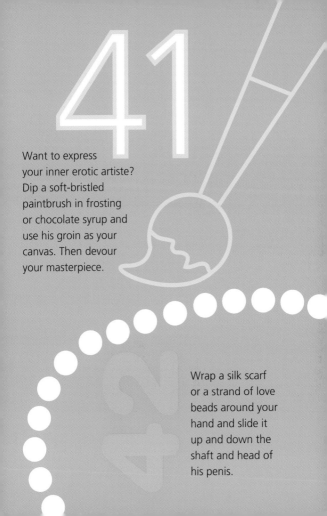

Section Three

Lucky Stiff

Variety's always welcome in the land down under (unless it involves sharp objects). The trick lies in knowing how to branch out from your basic slide-lick-suck and work his other bits into the action in a way that is most likely to make him your love slave. Hint: It's all about the build-up. Too much too soon and he could end up losing his concentration while too little too late and you could end up down there until the next millennium. So start small and finish big. Be warned: Perfect these beg-for-mercy manoeuvres and he may never want to get out of bed!

Ball Play

It's time to play with the family jewels.

43

Put both his balls in your mouth at once. Use one hand to circle the top of the sac and gently pull down to bring the balls together into a neat easy-to-swallow package. Then gently suck, hum a little tune and twirl with your tongue.

44

As you give his wicket your oral best, reach up and gently pull on his balls, working your hands in tandem with your mouth moves to virtually double the sensation.

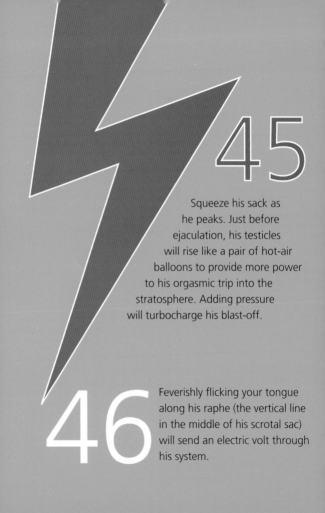

45

Squeeze his sack as he peaks. Just before ejaculation, his testicles will rise like a pair of hot-air balloons to provide more power to his orgasmic trip into the stratosphere. Adding pressure will turbocharge his blast-off.

46

Feverishly flicking your tongue along his raphe (the vertical line in the middle of his scrotal sac) will send an electric volt through his system.

47

Lightly graze your fingernails over his balls and the crease between his thigh and groin. For the first few seconds, barely touch him. As he gets used to the sensation – and his penis starts straightening up – apply more pressure (never scratching!), running the smooth tops of your nails forward and back. Take care: One misplaced talon could wreak havoc.

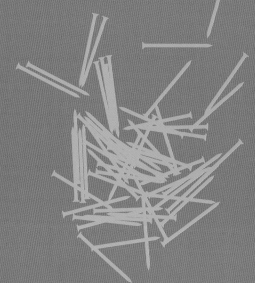

Get In the Zone

Let your mouth roam over the hottest places on and around his penis.

Give his love warrior a tongue lashing it'll never forget. Plant big wet ones over every inch of him. Start by pressing your tongue against the tip of the glans. Then tap it repeatedly against his fraenulum and press it flat against the sides of his hard-on using sweeping strokes as you lick up and down. Do it again... and again. By the third cycle, he'll either be convinced he's died and gone to heaven or he'll have passed out from utter joy.

48

His bottom isn't a black hole to be avoided at all costs. It's actually packed with sensitive nerves just begging for licking. Sweep his backfield with a stiff tongue. If you can't get beyond the bog factor, slip a cut-up condom over the area (the extra material may even boost the sensation). But check out tips 84 to 85 for info on washing behind his ears and tip 86 for the inside track on STIs (sexually transmitted infections) before hitting on his back door.

50

Play with his prostate and watch him prostrate himself before you. Hard to reach, this internal walnut-size gland is a pleasure minefield. Wrapping your lips (and hand, if necessary) around the shaft of his penis and, rather than doing your usual up-and-down thing, moving it toward his body will treat him to an inner massage.

To knead him into orgasmic oblivion, work your fingers against his perineum as you mouth him off.

51

Tongue Twisters

Nine tantalizing tactics that will keep him coming... back for more.

52

While moving up his shaft with your mouth, shake your head from side to side (as if you're saying no), letting your tongue follow a corkscrew pattern. Repeat, moving down his shaft.

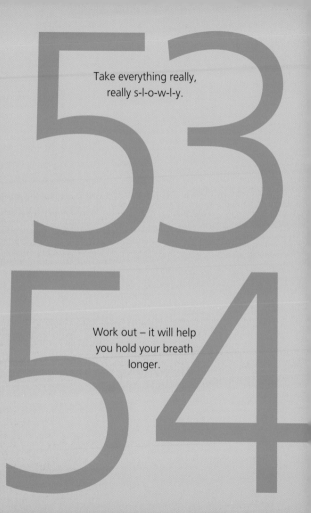

53

Take everything really, really s-l-o-w-l-y.

54

Work out – it will help you hold your breath longer.

55

Give him a hummer. Simply go "mmmm" for a few seconds on the head of his penis. Work your range: A low pitch makes slow vibrations; a higher one speeds things up.

56

Try this Taoist twist: Go shallow for nine bobs, go deep on the tenth. Then repeat the pattern, but this time do eight shallow bobs and two deep ones. Continue until you've worked your way down to one shallow bob and nine incredibly deep ones. Then do the shimmy, shimmy shake and get into his groove.

Do almost-oral sex where you get real close to his swag and then pass by with just a hot breath. Ignore his pleas. After about five of the longest minutes of his life, gobble him up.

57 58

Use your tongue to trace letters on his wee-wee for great initial stimulation. The pointed, firm tongue strokes will have him screaming for you to dot the "I".

59

Melt him faster than ice in a desert with long, slow tongue drags from bottom to top (like licking an ice lolly). Flatten your tongue to get the most surface-to-surface.

While deep-throating won't necessarily boost his pleasure Q (the most sensitive part of his little friend is the head), it will boost his estimation of your oral powers. Here's how to swallow his sword without messing up your lipstick.

- Pay attention to the angle of his dangle – work from above with an up-curving penis and below with a down-pointing one.

- If you gag easily, point him slightly toward the side of your throat instead of straight down. He won't go in as deep but he'll never notice the difference.

- Stop and relax your throat muscles every ½ in (1.3 cm) or so before letting him go deeper.

- Swallow – when his wand tickles the back your throat, that is. It will help gag your gag reflex and widen things.

On the Side

Here are eight treats you can add to the main menu to make things even more delicious.

61

Men are visually stimulated so give him a feast for his eyes by keeping the lights on so he can see his penis move in and out of your mouth.

62

Give him a wash 'n' dry. First, blow him with your mouth and then blow him with a hairdryer set on low.

63

Apply some bright red lipstick before lipping him off (it double-duties as a great lube).

64

Do him in a car. If possible, a red convertible. Preferably when he is not driving.

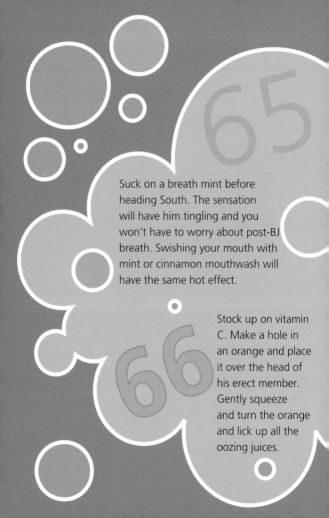

65

Suck on a breath mint before heading South. The sensation will have him tingling and you won't have to worry about post-BJ breath. Swishing your mouth with mint or cinnamon mouthwash will have the same hot effect.

66

Stock up on vitamin C. Make a hole in an orange and place it over the head of his erect member. Gently squeeze and turn the orange and lick up all the oozing juices.

67

Take a sip of water, tilting your head backward so it stays in the back of your throat and then take him in your mouth. Ice-cold water will send shivers down his spine while hot (but not scalding) liquid will fire him up.

68

Run an ice cube up and down his pole.

Section Four

The Big Gulp

Spit or swallow? For most blokes, it's a non-starter. The way they see it, their bodies have been working to produce that brew all day long. It's good stuff. But you may need a few more reasons. Try these on for size.

- Despite appearances, it's only about a teaspoon of semen.
- It's low-calorie and brimming with nutrients.
- The vitamin E content will give your skin a healthy glow.
- Unlike spitting, it's no muss or fuss so you can orally surprise him just about anywhere.

Ready? Here's how to go with his flow.

Blast-off

We've got lift-off. Here's how to prepare so you're not caught with your jaw hanging open.

If his penis swells, his body tenses and his balls draw close to his body, he's gonna blow (shouts of "I'm cooooommming" are also a dead give-away). Instantly recall what he does with his body during his intercourse orgasms – does he start jackhammering or does he stay slow and steady? Try mimicking the action with your mouth.

70

The second his flares go off, up the stimulation by pressing firmly against his perineum.

If you want to bring him around for Round Two when he's already climaxed, caress his ding-dong lightly with your tongue.

71

Cocktail Party

How to swallow without gagging, making faces or saying "yuck".

Want to know what his semen will taste like without swallowing a drop? Check his diet.

- Too much fast food or spicy and salty snacks can give him a pungent zest.
- An overindulgence of booze, coffee and ciggies may lead to a bad taste in your mouth.
- Asparagus, broccoli, onions and garlic add a bitter note to his character.

Bland foods like pasta, fruit and potatoes will keep his taste finger lickin' good. Heads up: If he used to taste differently, he may have an STI such as trichomoniasis or chlamydia. You'll both need to get checked out by a doctor immediately (study up on poison penises in tip 86).

Get a taster. When he's hot to trot, his Cowper's glands (located at the base of his penis) produce a liquid that lubes his urethra so semen can blast through fancy free. This stuff tastes a lot like the real thing and leaks in manageable dribbles just before he ejaculates.

73

When you sense he's about to come (refresh your memory with tip 69 – heh-heh), angle him so that his shooting end is pointing at your cheek instead of straight down your throat.

75

Dentistry isn't exactly a romantic profession, but a recent study on oral pain and acupressure found that if he puts the first three fingers of his hand together and presses them against the inside of your wrist (aka the P-6 region) while simultaneously poking around your mouth, the gag reflect diminishes considerably.

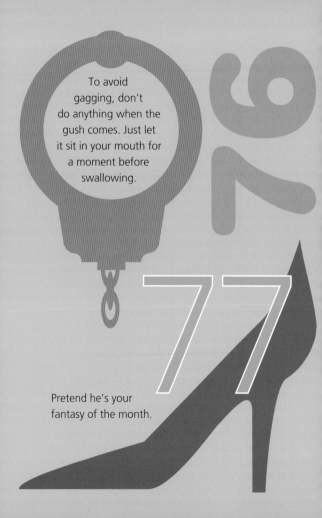

76

To avoid gagging, don't do anything when the gush comes. Just let it sit in your mouth for a moment before swallowing.

77

Pretend he's your fantasy of the month.

Clean Finish

Ditch the spit kit. There are lots of things you can do with his semen besides swallowing it.

Give him a dry orgasm. Contrary to popular belief, a man's orgasm and his ejaculation are an inseparable team. A study at the State University of New York Health Science Center at Brooklyn found that men can actually learn to climax three to ten times before ejaculating by flexing their pubococcygeal muscle (the one he uses to control his pee flow).

78

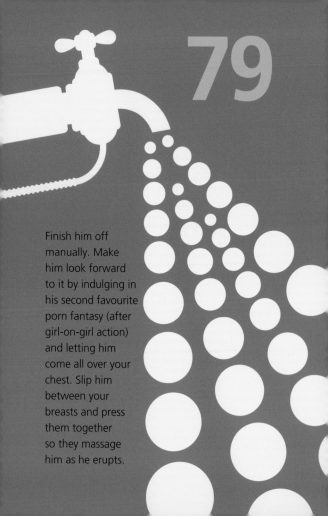

79

Finish him off manually. Make him look forward to it by indulging in his second favourite porn fantasy (after girl-on-girl action) and letting him come all over your chest. Slip him between your breasts and press them together so they massage him as he erupts.

80

If you finish him off by hand, add some water-based lube to give your digits the warmth and wetness of your mouth.

Don't put your mouth out of action completely. You can still lick the general area while you move over to manhandling him. Make sure you have some tissues or a towel nearby to wipe up the spillage.

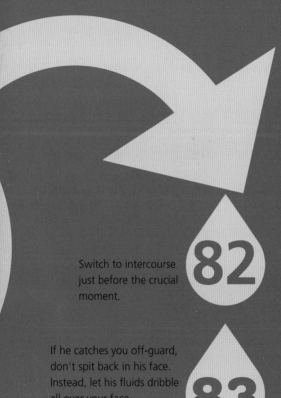

Switch to intercourse just before the crucial moment.

82

If he catches you off-guard, don't spit back in his face. Instead, let his fluids dribble all over your face.

83

Section Five

BJ
Blunders

Any man lucky enough to be on the receiving
end of your marvellous mouth magic should
show the proper grace and appreciation (or, at the
very least, reciprocation). So, if he pushes your head
down or holds it in a vice-like grip, caution him
with a little tooth action. Also, remind him that
your ears are not handles. And no, do not do
him while he watches the game.

Read on for other ways to help him
mind his manners.

Poison Penises

Hopefully you won't accidentally bump into
any of these snake charmers in the dark.

IT SMELLS FUNKY:

- A dusting of cornstarch will keep stinky sweat from
  festering down there during the day and be gone by
  the time you want to nose around.
- If he has a stinky or sour odour that doesn't disappear
  once he showers, either he needs to adjust his diet
  (does he relish anything in tip 72?) or he has an
  infection (proceed instantly to tip 86) or a smegma
  build-up (see tip 85 below). If it's just the way he tastes,
  check out tip 35 to see how he can sweeten up his act.

IT LOOKS DIRTY:

- If you can't get it out of your head that he pees and
  comes with the same tool, send him to the showers
  before giving him an oral bath...
- Or you can work him into a lather by soaping him
  down yourself.
- **Uncut Version:** Smegma, a cheesy substance, can
  form under the loose flap of skin if he doesn't wash
  behind his little guy's ears. Pull back his foreskin and
  gently wipe.

85

IT'S TOXIC:

- The average guy has a 60% chance of being infected with a sexually transmitted infection (STI).

- While penile skin is often bumpy (naturally or because he has sebaceous cysts of hair follicles, an allergic reaction or pearly penile papules – all of which are nothing to worry about), it may also mean he has HPV (human papilloma virus or genital warts), MCV (molluscum contagiosum virus), syphilis or herpes – all infections you can catch through skin-to-skin contact.

- HIV, hepatitis B, hepatitis C and cytomegalovirus (CMV) can also be passed orally. And if you have a cold sore, you can pass this infection onto his willy and he may then develop full-blown genital herpes.

- Bottom Line: Until you both get a clean bill of health from a doctor, don't go near his naked penis (look opposite for the lowdown on using a condom).

- If you have even the slightest question about his penis health, dress him up in a condom first. Skip the prelubricated kinds, which tend to have a bad taste and opt for a more lickable one, flavoured like fruit or candy, instead.

- **Uncut Version:** Max out on the sensation he feels when using a condom by making sure the foreskin is completely pulled back before rolling on the rubber.

- If you both have a clean bill of health, perfect the ultimate party trick by slipping him into his rubbers with your mouth (a reversible polyurethane like eZ-on is designed to unfold in either direction, so you don't need to worry about accidentally contaminating the business side). Once he has a little backbone, hold the condom very gently in your mouth with the opening facing out. Take a deep breath to create suction and then, using your tongue to help, gently roll it down your lover's penis with your lips (practice on a banana first).

IT'S HAIRY:

- No one likes to find hair in the meal. He's probably never once thought about below-the-belt hair grooming. But tell him that not only will a trim give you better access to his shaft, it will also make him look bigger – and watch how fast he starts snipping.

- Make his buzz cut part of your erotic play. Use an electric beard clipper or bikini trimmer to add some sweet vibrations.

Speed Him Up

Blowjobs can occasionally be a lot of work (hence the name). If you're at the point where your mind is wandering and wondering whether that cute bag you want to buy went on sale yet, don't throw in the towel. Here are five things guaranteed to send him into happy oblivion in less time than it takes to say, "Are you close to coming?"

Work all his bits and pieces at the same time (see tips 28 to 32 for ideas).

89

Drop everything and zone in on his fraenulum. This ultrasensitive area is like a male clitoris – packed with nerve endings, it's a no-fail big-O trigger. With every lick, add a little extra tongue pressure in that one spot until he climaxes.

Wrap your thumb and index finger around the shaft, about 1 in (2.5 cm) above the base, and pull down while sucking down on the head. He'll probably climax in two minutes tops.

Launch sequence still not happening? Give it up and make him come another way – with your hand or via intercourse. Save face by sighing, "You made me so hot I can't wait to feel you inside of me."

26

If your mouth is tired, stick your tongue out as far as you can and press down. Now you can use your neck muscles instead, and you'll be able to stay the course without getting tongue-tied.

Slow Him Down

Of course, if he comes fast it may just mean that you are very, very good. However, it also means he may now roll over and fall into a post-O coma. To slow him down to your climatic time, unashamedly try one (or more) of the following tricks.

93

When you sense that he's reaching his pleasure peak (see tip 69 for clues), stop touching him completely for 30 seconds. That should be enough time for him to get in control of himself.

Take matters into
your own hands and firmly
press his secret off-spot – the
cushy area between the scrotum
and the anus – counting one-
elephant, two-elephant and so
on until you get to five.

94

Slip a ring on him. Not a wedding ring (although that may also cool his heels), but a cock ring. It will trap blood in the penis, which means he's yours for as long as you want him (20 minutes is the max to avoid damaging the capillaries and bruising the penis).

Try a style that goes on easily (even after he's hardened up) and can be adjusted and taken off, like a Velcro ring (see tip 35 for resources). The tighter you make it, the more intense the release.

96

Tell him that male participation is required in this event. If he's lying back and doing nothing, casually mention that if he gives you a reason to enjoy going South of his belly border, you'll keep coming back for more.

It Takes Two to Tango

A BJ doesn't have to be a one-way road. Here, for your reading pleasure, are five things he can do to you to while you do him.

Position yourself over him so he has easy access to your bits and pieces – and no excuses. And because you're on top, you can decide when to pause for moans (but don't leave him hanging – continue working him over with your hands).

If his hands on you is too much of a distraction for you to give proper attention to the (blow)job at hand, suggest he redirects his touches. He may not be able to press your love button but he can still play with your hair, stroke your face, run his fingers over your back and knead your shoulders.

99

Ask him to hold your hair back out of your face (added incentive – he'll get a better view of the action).

100

Remind him there is no such thing as too much flattery. Anything along the lines of "You look so sexy between my legs," "I love and adore you" and "You give the best head I ever received" should guarantee him a second below-the-belt round.